CULTURE+TYPOGRAPHY
how culture affects typography

NIKKI VILLAGOMEZ

Cincinnati, Ohio
www.howdesign.com

CULTURE + TYPOGRPAPHY. Copyright © 2015 by Nikki Villagomez. Manufactured in China. All rights reserved. No other part of this book may be reproduced in any form or by any electronic or mechanical means including information storage and retrieval systems without permission in writing from the publisher, except by a reviewer, who may quote brief passages in a review. Published by PRINT Books, an imprint of F+W, a Content + Ecommerce Company, 10151 Carver Road, Suite 200, Blue Ash, Ohio 45242. (800) 289-0963. First edition.

For more excellent books and resources for designers, visit www.printmag.com.

19 18 17 16 15   5 4 3 2 1

ISBN-13: 978-1-4403-3841-0

Distributed in Canada by Fraser Direct
100 Armstrong Avenue
Georgetown, Ontario, Canada L7G 5S4
Tel: (905) 877-4411
Distributed in the U.K. and Europe by F&W Media International, LTD
Brunel House, Forde Close, Newton Abbot, TQ12 4PU, UK
Tel: (+44) 1626 323200, Fax: (+44) 1626 323319
Email: enquiries@fwmedia.com
Distributed in Australia by Capricorn Link
P.O. Box 704, Windsor, NSW 2756 Australia
Tel: (02) 4560-1600

fw
a content + ecommerce company

Edited by Scott Francis
Cover design by Claudean Wheeler
Interior design by Hannah Bailey
Production coordinated by Greg Nock
Typography set in Aptifter Slab LT Pro and Aptifer Sans LT Pro by Mårten Thavenius

Dedication

Eduardo. Kai Rodrigo. Ayla Eaves. My perfectly kerned family.

Acknowledgments

With any major undertaking, there are people that need to be recognized for help, support and encouragement that I received along the way. I have to start by thanking HOW for giving me this wonderful opportunity. Writing a book has been a long term goal of mine that I'm so excited see come to fruition.

I am very grateful for the support from my company Dixon Hughes Goodman LLP (DHG) and my wonderful co-workers. Their constant encouragement, high fives and genuine interest has meant the world to me. My blog (www.nikkivillagomez.wordpress.com) has been the catalyst for this book has served as my personal inspirational portal these last few years and because of that, I know I am a better designer professionally.

My parents, my foundation, Emile and Donna Rasheed, deserve my endless thanks and gratitude for their unwavering support and positive feedback. Thanks to my brother, Charly Rasheed, for always offering advise, kind words of encouragment and for keeping that sock on.

Lastly, my husband and best friend, Eduardo Villagomez, for always pushing me to be better and do better. One of the most important things that I have learned throughout this whole experience is that it's so much more rewarding doing what you love with the people you love. I can safely say that my love for typography is, on good days, an obsession. Even though my husband is not a type lover like me, he has always been willing to go letterhunting (with minimal eye roll), help me prepare for my speaking engagements, and listen to me go into minute detail about everything that happened when I return from my trips. None of this would have been possible without his love and support. It also doesn't hurt to have our two kids cheering me on (with not so minimal eye roll!). Thank you Kai and Ayla for being on this journey with me.

PHOTO CREDIT: iMADEFACE, KEYLOFT INC.

About the Author

Nikki Villagomez is a nationally recognized speaker on typography. She is a graduate of Louisiana State University with a BFA in graphic design. After working as a designer in New York City for several years, she moved to her home state of South Carolina where she became a fulltime freelancer. Nikki is the founder and former president of the South Carolina chapter of AIGA. She has taught Graphic Design and Typography at the University of South Carolina and the University of Akron. Currently, Nikki is the creative studio manager at Dixon Hughes Goodman LLP (DHG) in Charlotte, North Carolina. In her free time, she maintains her blog (nikkivillagomez.wordpress.com) about how culture affects typography.

FIND ME HERE:  nikkivillagomez.wordpress.com @nikki_vz nikki_vz nikkivillagomez@gmail.com

Table of Contents

INTRODUCTION..01

01 | GHOST SIGNS..04

02 | MANHOLE COVERS..36

03 | GRAFFITI..54

04 | HAND-LETTERING..82

05 | SIGNAGE..110

06 | NEON SIGNS..140

07 | WAYFINDING...170

08 | CULTURAL OBSERVATIONS...190

Introduction

I consider myself fortunate that I can pinpoint exactly what inspires me. It took me a while to get here, but the journey was worth it.

In September 2004, I founded the South Carolina chapter of the American Institute of Graphic Arts (AIGA). My goal during the two years I served as president, was to hold monthly events that were inspirational and beneficial for the local design community. While we garnered a national reputation for our speaker series, there was one event that had the most impact for me personally. December is a low key month for events due to the holidays, but I still wanted to keep the momentum and energy behind our chapter going. A few months prior to our chapter launching, I had made friends with the president of the AIGA Honolulu chapter at the AIGA Leadership Retreat. After I made a fool of myself freaking out that she lived in Hawaii (which, of course, was my dream destination), I regained my composure and said, "Since I have no chance of going to Hawaii anytime soon, wouldn't it be neat if we did a culture exchange?!"

The concept was simple: AIGA SC boxed up anything and everything that had to do with South Carolina (a bag of grits, bumper stickers from the University of South Carolina, decals from Clemson University, tea grown in Charleston, our state flag, etc.) as well as pieces designed by South Carolina designers for the clients from our state. I hung South Carolina fun facts off of each piece that was sent. We shipped the box to Hawaii in exchange for a box from AIGA Honolulu. And for our December event, we opened the box from Hawaii and explored their culture.

They did a great job sending Hawaii to South Carolina. There was a Hawaiian sound track for us to listen to as we made our discoveries, everyone got leis and there was sand from Waikiki! As awesome as all that was, what got my attention the most were the pieces designed by Hawaiian designers for Hawaiian clients. I was blown away by how much their culture affects their design, and it forced me to look at design in a completely different way. Font selection, color usage, and other design choices were inspired by the visual language of their cultural surroundings. Was this a conscious choice or was it intuitive? The following year we worked with the AIGA Las Vegas chapter on another exchange. Once again, I was blown away by the completely different styles of design reflective of the Vegas vibe. The experience reminded me to always be keenly aware of design when I travel, to really observe the design around me and notice how culture has played a part in the choices that have been made—specifically with the typography.

Over the years, these two culture exchanges have stayed with me. As an Adjunct Instructor at the University of South Carolina, my love for graphic design and my passion for typography were being met without me even realizing it. As I made the transition from being an educator to an in-house designer, I only then realized I needed an outlet for my typography love..

As much as I love what I do for a living, I quickly realized that what inspires me the most is typography.

So my outlet became my blog (https://nikkivillagomez.wordpress.com). My goal is to bring awareness to typography and how culture plays a part in the choices that are made—this was directly inspired by the two culture exchange events. On my blog, I post side-by-side comparisons of pictures from different parts of the world that highlight how the typography landscape varies.

I'm a firm believer in setting goals, so as I embarked on the journey of blogging, I set four goals for myself:

1. Post five days a week.
2. Don't let the blog interfere with my work or my family.
3. Do it for me (ignore negative comments, how much traffic the site gets, etc.).
4. As soon as it becomes a chore, pull the plug.

So, I started my blog with my first post on July 14, 2011 and never looked back. On May 17, 2012 I had my first speaking engagement with the AIGA Richmond chapter with a talk titled How Culture Affects Typography, I asked local creatives to take pictures of the typography that makes Richmond unique and send them to me one month prior to my talk. I used these pictures to put together a presentation that was specific to Richmond and show just how unique the city is. Since Richmond event wrapped, I have taken my talk to the AIGA chapters of Cleveland, South Carolina (Columbia), Atlanta, Cincinnati, San Antonio, Orlando, South Dakota (Sioux Falls), Upstate New York (Syracuse), Connecticut (New Haven), Miami, Austin and New Mexico. I had set a goal for myself when I was a sophmore studying graphic design at Louisiana State University that one day, I would be a speaker at the HOW Design Live Conference. Seventeen years later, on May 15, 2014, I reached that goal as one of the speakers for the conference which was held in Boston, Massachusetts. All of this spun off from my love of typography.

It is my routine the morning after each talk to wake up stupid early and walk around whatever city I am in. I explore what each city has to offer and experience the culture first hand. I carry a point-and-shoot camera and my iPhone with me to document my findings. I don't claim to be a professional photographer; I just capture what catches my eye. I will be forever grateful to the AIGA chapters across the country that have provided me with such a wonderful opportunity to travel to cities I probably wouldn't have seen otherwise, but meeting fellow designers and creatives in different cities has been the most rewarding aspect of this experience. I have formed valuable friendships that I'm truly grateful for. As I continue to set goals for myself for the future, these kinds of speaking engagements remain on my list.

It is important to note that the pictures in this book are limited to the places I have been fortunate enough to visit and are based on my own experiences and what has inspired me along the way. As you are reading through, I'm hopeful that you will be inspired to really look at what the typography around you has to offer and find your own inspiration. Throughout my travels, I have come to realize:

SIOUX FALLS, SOUTH DAKOTA

The culture that lives in a city is like a virus that is trying to stay alive.

SIOUX FALLS, SOUTH DAKOTA

I mean the word *virus* in the best way possible. As I travel, I am always in search of this virus, the culture that's clinging for dear life, so I can document it through pictures and then record it on my blog. This book is a celebration of my discoveries.

The best example that I have come across of what I mean by "culture that is trying to stay alive" is Crawford's Bar & Grill in downtown Sioux Falls, South Dakota. I went to Crawford's for dinner with a few of the AIGA South Dakota board members and immediately fell in love with the lettering of the logo. After doing some research, I found out that the building started out as a butcher shop in 1896. It was later converted to a store in the 1930s, and in 1963, the Crawford's Men's Wear logo was designed and placed in the floor at the store entrance (above). When the Crawford's building later became a bar and grill, the owners could have completely rebranded their restaurant, but instead they opted to incorporate the original logo into their branding (opposite page). Inside the restaurant, there are even nods to the original butcher shop. Black soot stains a portion of the wall where the meat was smoked and a blood trough runs along the north cellar wall—beautiful ways to preserve the history in a corner of the city.

01 GHOST SIGNS

SYRACUSE, NEW YORK

6 • CHAPTER ONE

A ghost sign is an advertisment that has been preserved on a building for an extended period of time. The sign (hand painted, floor tiles or neon signs) may be kept for its nostalgic appeal, or simply indifference by the owner. Most of the ghost signs I have come across advertise a product or service that isn't specific to the area (just like most billboards or ads that are commonly found today). The ghost signs are interesting because of their age, but I don't always find that they offer true insight into the culture of the area in which they are located in. The ghost signs on these two pages are particularly interesting because they have the city name in which they were found.

Here's an interesting lesson you can learn from studying ghost signs: Achieving a different look with typography, can be accomplished by simply changing your medium. Notice the different forms the letters are forced to take from the grid of the tiled entryways compared to more free hand-lettered signs on the sides of buildings.

QUICK TIP

Collecting your own typograpy photos? When uploading pictures to your computer, open them in Photoshop and adjust the brightness/contrast tool to help with legibility. From your Adjustments pull down menu, go to the Brightness/Contrast tool and preview your work as you go for optimum legibility.

SAN ANTONIO, TEXAS

RICHMOND, VIRGINIA

SAN ANTONIO, TEXAS

PITTSBURGH, PENNSYLVANIA

NASHVILLE, TENNESSEE

CLEVELAND, OHIO

SIOUX FALLS, SOUTH DAKOTA

SYRACUSE, NEW YORK

CUYAHOGA FALLS, OHIO

Who used ghost signs to advertise?

Businesses of all types and sizes once used hand-painted advertising to publicize themselves. These included smaller local companies who may have had signs painted on their premises, all the way up to big brands such as Gillette and Hovis who paid for signs all across the United Kingdom. There are also many examples of signs that have outlived the company or product being advertising. So just imagine the vast array of typography examples you can explore by examining these reminders of days gone by.

CINCINNATI, OHIO

AUSTIN, TEXAS

The type that sits on the tops of buildings is a treasure. You never know what is lurking up there, but it's almost always bound to be something interesting. Much like the beautiful typography that can be found on gravestones, the older the building, the more unusual the letters and numbers are likely to be.

The Wilson Building in Syracuse, New York was undergoing a rennovation during my visit. The building's hand-painted (2-D) ghost sign first caught my attention as I turned the street corner (below left), but it paled in comparison to the lettering and abbreviation above the main entrance (right). Not to be outdone is the Vermont Building in Boston, Massachusetts (opposite page). While there's nothing fancy going on with the letters, check out the apostrophes! Why have one when you can have two?!

SYRACUSE, NEW YORK

ORLANDO, FLORIDA

BOSTON, MASSACHUSETTS

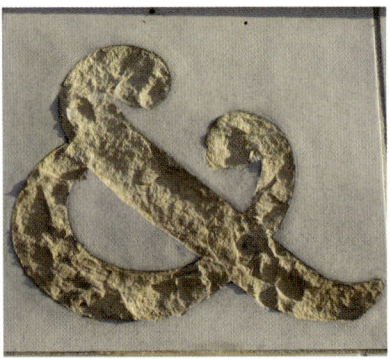 

SYRACUSE, NEW YORK

The Tinker Building was built in 1925 by the legendary baseball icon Joseph B. Tinker to house his real estate business. In 1980 it was added to the National Register of Historic Places.

ORLANDO, FLORIDA

The Frick & Lindsay Building, which opened in 1902, is also listed on the National Register of Historic Places. It has been the home to the Andy Warhol Museum since 1994. Both of these have similar type styles, but notice the type is set completely differently. As a result the signs have a very different feel.

PITTSBURGH, PENNSYLVANIA

AKRON, OHIO

WOOSTER, OHIO

BOSTON, MASSACHUSETTS

CLEVELAND, OHIO

ATLANTA, GEORGIA

NASHVILLE, TENNESSEE

SYRACUSE, NEW YORK

GREENVILLE, SOUTH CAROLINA

CLEVELAND, OHIO

GHOST SIGNS

This Tower sign appears to have once been part of a neon sign that has since fallen apart. The portion with the four colored boxes at the bottom seems to have gone through an identity crisis. You can just make out the word *JUMP* behind the newer type.

It's always amusing to see how apostrophes get handled in vertical signs. In the case of Tucker's Restaurant (below, right), it gets its own line! It's such a contrast to see the spaced out lettering of *Tucker's* to the jam packed *Restaurant*.

I drove past this abandonded bar in Columbus, Ohio (opposite page) and slammed on my brakes to turn around and take pictures. I got an ear full of honking car horns, but as far as I'm concerned, it was totally worth it.

Whenever you find yourself in need of inspiration for a project, look to the vintage signs in the world around you. It's amazing the level of detail and interesting typography and color choices that can be discovered!

The Cincinnati Color Building, built in the 1950's, has been renovated since I took this picture. The sign remains and has been refurbished, including a new coat of paint.

CINCINNATI, OHIO

COLUMBUS, OHIO

SIOUX FALLS, SOUTH DAKOTA

SALEM, OHIO

RICHMOND, VIRGINIA

SAN ANTONIO, TEXAS

18 • CHAPTER ONE

SAN ANTONIO, TEXAS

This bakery sign is a great example of the power of contrast. The right typeface can even make concrete look like soft and maliable pastry dough.

COLUMBIA, SOUTH CAROLINA

How were ghost signs produced?

These kinds of signs were painted by skilled craftsmen known as signwriters or, in some parts of the U.S., *walldogs*. While the work available has been in significant decline, some are still plying the trade. There are many different techniques employed in producing the signs and each signwriter would have carried out the task in a different way. Smaller signs could be produced freehand, sometimes using the mortar lines in the brick to measure the height of the letters. Another common method was using a spiked wheel to perforate the lines of a design into a sheet of paper. This could then be placed on the wall and patted with charcoal or chalk dust to leave an outline which could be filled in with paint. Depending on the skill of the signwriter, and the budget of the client, a sign could include many flourishes including illustrations and other decorative elements.

PITTSBURGH, PENNSYLVANIA

NEW YORK CITY, NEW YORK

NASHVILLE, TENNESSEE

CLEVELAND, OHIO

ALBUQUERQUE, NEW MEXICO

22 • CHAPTER ONE

RICHMOND, VIRGINIA

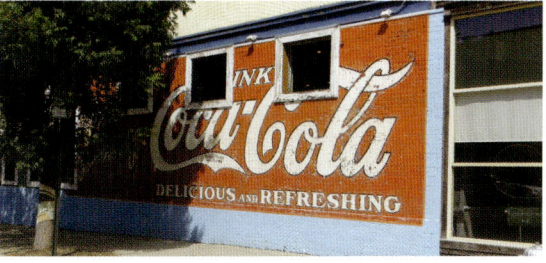

ATLANTA, GEORGIA

GREENVILLE, SOUTH CAROLINA

SYRACUSE, NEW YORK

CLEVELAND, OHIO

BOSTON, MASSACHUSETTS

RICHMOND, VIRGINIA

PITTSBURGH, PENNSYLVANIA

01

GHOST SIGNS

CINCINNATI, OHIO

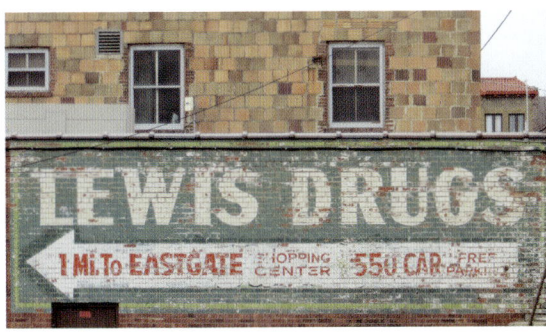

SIOUX FALLS, SOUTH DAKOTA　　　**COLUMBIA, SOUTH CAROLINA**　　　**PHOENIX, ARIZONA**

CLEVELAND, OHIO

CINCINNATI, OHIO

PITTSBURGH, PENNSYLVANIA

ST. LOUIS, MISSOURI

Where are ghost signs most commonly found?

There are examples of ghost signs all across the world including France, Australia, the United States, the UK and Netherlands. While these countries provide lots of examples from the past you can also find fresh signs being painted in many parts of the world including India, Mexico, Jamaica, Cambodia and Bangladesh. In more developed countries they tend to be most common in former industrial centres, although you will also find them in the smallest country villages. The key to finding them is paying attention to the buildings you pass and looking up as they are often situated high on the walls.

PITTSBURGH, PENNSYLVANIA

We've spent some time looking up. Now it's time to look down. Let's examine some typography found in the floor at the entrance to stores–that no longer advertises the current business (if there is a business at all). What has been the most interesting to observe with these signs is the effect a grid (due to the tile work) has on the letters. Most of the examples are sans serif type treatments (below, left), which makes sense as it is the easiest to put the letters in place. Things start to get crazy when serifs are introduced (below, right) or *really* crazy when script is introduced (bottom of page.)

SIOUX FALLS, SOUTH DAKOTA

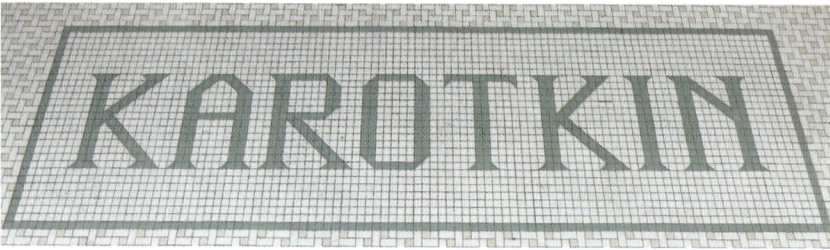

AUSTIN, TEXAS

CINCINNATI, OHIO

NASHVILLE, TENNESSEE

One of my most interesting finds is this lone apostrophe that remains after the rest of the sign was covered up. Someone took the time to retile this entrance to get rid of the letters that used to be here, but they didn't want to spend the extra money to get rid of the four and a half tiles that make up the apostrophe.

CINCINNATI, OHIO

MIAMI, FLORIDA

ORLANDO, FLORIDA

SAN ANTONIO, TEXAS

SYRACUSE, NEW YORK

CHARLESTON, SOUTH CAROLINA

FREDERICKSBURG, VIRGINIA

NEW YORK CITY, NEW YORK

NEW HAVEN, CONNECTICUT

GREENVILLE, SOUTH CAROLINA

SAN FRANCISCO, CALIFORNIA

GHOST SIGNS

S. H. Kress & Co. was a chain of five and dime stores that operated from 1896 to 1981. The first of the stores was opened by Samuel H. Kress in Nanticoke, Pennsylvania in 1887. It became a chain and during the first half of the twentieth century Kress stores were found on Main Streets of hundreds of towns across the country. In 1964 Kress was acquired by Genesco, Inc., who began moving the stores from Main Streets to shopping malls. Eventually the company began closing down the Kress stores in 1980. During its heyday, however, the Kress chain was known for the fine architecture of its buildings. A number of former Kress stores are recognized as architectural landmarks and many are listed on the National Register of Historic Places, including the 1935 building on Orange Avenue in Orlando (below, now Kress Chophouse.)

ORLANDO, FLORIDA

ALBUQUERQUE, NEW MEXICO

MIAMI, FLORIDA

ATLANTA, GEORGIA

GHOST SIGNS • 33

SAN ANTONIO, TEXAS

34 • CHAPTER ONE

YOUNGSTOWN, OHIO

02 MANHOLE COVERS

What's fascinating about manhole covers is how something that is so utilitarian can be so beautiful. Just like ghost signs, manholes that are specific to their city or state are much more interesting because they often reveal historical and cultural clues about the area. These kinds of manhole covers are unique and can offer interesting studies of letterforms and design patterns.

In regards to the typography, I have found that sans serif typefaces are most commonly utilized. This makes sense because the letters are easier to read, and they hold up better in the elements. With the sans serif typefaces, I have discovered more variety in the thickness of the letterforms and the spacing. When serifed typefaces are used, spacing is limited and thicker letterforms are the norm for legibility.

Here is a wide array of styles, and you're sure to find interesting textures—diamonds, squares, lines and circles are just a few of the components that make up some pretty intricate patterns. But also make sure to study the variety of letterforms here. You'll note fat type, skinny type, serifs and sans serifs—the more yowu look, the more variety you'll notice.

QUICK TIP

It might seem like an obvious suggestion, but make sure you look both ways before standing in the middle of a street to take a picture of a manhole cover. The fact that manholes are usually positioned in streets or sidewalks makes it imperative for you to be aware of your surroundings and traffic when conducting your studies. Also, be prepared for pedestrians to not take too kindly to you stopping abruptly in the middle of a sidewalk to take a picture.

CLEVELAND, OHIO

GREENVILLE, SOUTH CAROLINA

ORLANDO, FLORIDA

ALBUQUERQUE, NEW MEXICO

CLEVELAND, OHIO

AUSTIN, TEXAS

SIOUX FALLS, SOUTH DAKOTA

NASHVILLE, TENNESSEE

SYRACUSE, NEW YORK

BOSTON, MASSACHUSETTS

ORLANDO, FLORIDA

GREENVILLE, SOUTH CAROLINA

RICHMOND, VIRGINIA

SAN ANTONIO, TEXAS

FREDERICKSBURG, VIRGINIA

NEW HAVEN, CONNECTICUT

02 MANHOLE COVERS

ORLANDO, FLORIDA

SAN ANTONIO, TEXAS

ALBUQUERQUE, NEW MEXICO

AUSTIN, TEXAS

This spread shows manhole covers that are put in place by telephone companies. The only clue that they offer in regards to their location, if any at all, is a regional reference. This is a stark contrast to sewer drains and water meter covers, which are typically branded to the specific city they are in. It is interesting to note that the three covers on the bottom of the opposite page and the cover on the bottom of this page have the same pattern but the illustrations of the bells are very different.

SAN ANTONIO, TEXAS

BOSTON, MASSACHUSETTS

AUSTIN, TEXAS

SAN ANTONIO, TEXAS

BOSTON, MASSACHUSETTS

SIOUX FALLS, SOUTH DAKOTA

On sidewalks next to rain drains, you can often find little plaques embedded into the concrete reminding passersby to not throw trash down the drain. Ironically, you have to look carefully as they are easy to miss given their size. The examples on this page are all about the size of your hand or smaller. The illustrations of the animals that are on these plaques are often a fun representation of the animals that are specific to the area. In addition to the illustrations, there is often a tie to which lake or river the water drains to. In cities with a high Hispanic population, you will find both English and Spanish represented.

ALBUQUERQUE, NEW MEXICO

SIOUX FALLS, SOUTH DAKOTA   **SAN FRANCISCO, CALIFORNIA**   **FREDERICKSBURG, VIRGINIA**   **AUSTIN, TEXAS**

Some covers offer no details at all, they are just beautiful patterns, while others are very easy to miss. These three on the left are about the size of a quarter! While they aren't manhole covers, they do have the same properties. The two taken in Texas are markers placed within the concrete in the middle of a sidewalk--both incorporate the star from the Texas flag and one incorporates an image of the Alamo. The one taken in Connecticut was embedded within the structure of a metal steam grate. Tiny gems that are easy to miss if you aren't looking!

AUSTIN, TEXAS

SAN ANTONIO, TEXAS

NEW HAVEN, CONNECTICUT

SIOUX FALLS, SOUTH DAKOTA

SAN FRANCISCO, CALIFORNIA

GREENVILLE, SOUTH CAROLINA

ALBUQUERQUE, NEW MEXICO

Water covers are some of the most beautiful examples that I have come across because they are so unique. They come in all shapes and sizes, including these two (below) that *are* manhole covers (in contrast to the markers from the previous page). These are also about the size of a quarter!

BOSTON, MASSACHUSETTS

AUSTIN, TEXAS

AKRON, OHIO

SAN ANTONIO, TEXAS

SAN FRANCISCO, CALIFORNIA

NEW HAVEN, CONNECTICUT

ATLANTA, GEORGIA

CUYAHOGA FALLS, OHIO

SAN ANTONIO, TEXAS

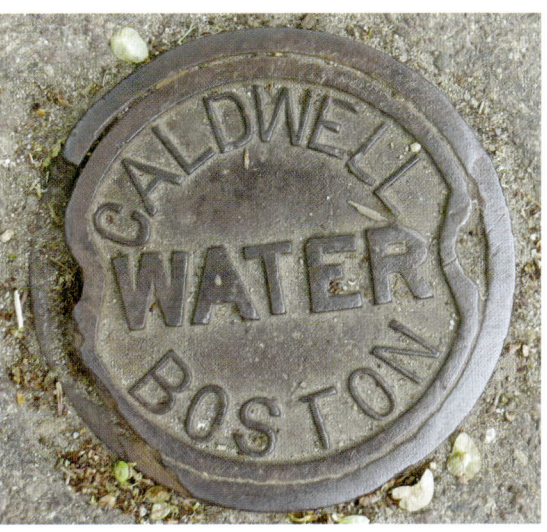

BOSTON, MASSACHUSETTS

ALBUQUERQUE, NEW MEXICO

GREENVILLE, SOUTH CAROLINA

SAN FRANCISCO, CALIFORNIA

WHY ARE THE MAJORITY OF MANHOLE COVERS ROUND?

- A round manhole cover cannot fall through its circular opening, whereas a square manhole cover may fall in if it were inserted diagonally in the hole.
- Round tubes are the strongest and most material-efficient shape against the compression of the earth around them, and so it is natural that the cover of a round tube assume a circular shape.
- A round manhole cover has a smaller surface than a square one, thus less material is needed to cast the manhole cover, meaning lower cost.
- The bearing surfaces of manhole frames and covers are machined to assure flatness and prevent them from becoming dislodged by traffic. Round castings are much easier to machine using a lathe.
- Circular covers do not need to be rotated to align with the manhole and they can be moved easily by being rolled.
- A round manhole cover can be easily locked in place with a quarter turn (as is done in countries like France). They are then hard to open without a special tool. Also, they do not have to be made so heavy because traffic passing over them cannot lift them up by suction.

QUICK TIP

If you come across letters that you find interesting, do rubbings of them and then scan them in for future inspiration.

While my main focus when I'm traveling is to observe how culture effects typography, seeing the effects that outside factors like weather and traffic can have on letters is just as interesting. Here are some of my favorite examples of the way letters start to deteriorate. Some hold their shape relatively well; others aren't as fortunate—but the result is beautiful. The breakdown of the letterforms tends to be more obvious and dramatic in the san serif letterforms set in a thinner typeface.

BOSTON, MASSACHUSETTS

SAN ANTONIO, TEXAS

ATLANTA, GEORGIA

RICHMOND, VIRGINIA

AKRON, OHIO

03 GRAFFITI

Graffiti is more than just urban art that has been scribbled, scratched, or sprayed illicitly on a public surface. Consisting of anything from simple written words to elaborate wall paintings, graffiti has existed since ancient times, with examples dating back to ancient Egypt, ancient Greece and the Roman Empire. It can offer enormous insight into art, fashion, culture and public opinion.

In addition to graffiti, there is also street art and urban art. While graffiti consists mostly of an artist tagging a wall with words or a stylized signature, street art often employs stencils, wheat-pasted posters and stickers. Urban art summarizes all visual art forms arising in an urban area, illicit or otherwise.

NEW YORK, NEW YORK

When studying typography to better understand how culture plays a role in the decisions that are made, you'll likely find that New York City is impossible to categorize. The city is a melting pot of all cultures and economic statuses—an organic creation of the people that reside there. Understandably, the city has a little bit of everything in terms of typography. It isn't dominant by any one thing like hand lettering, wayfinding, ghost signs or neon signs, but you can find unique examples of each just roaming the streets of Manhattan. New York City has it all, including killer street art.

NEW YORK, NEW YORK

Looking for cultural significance in graffiti is difficult as it's so random and diverse. But one can gain insight to a city's comings and goings based on where graffiti appears—on trains, bridges and in back alleys. It may not be reflective of the culture, but it works its way in and becomes one with the city. The flip side of this is commissioned artwork that is more refelective of their environment. Scenes like these can be found in any city, and offer an interesting contrast.

CLEVELAND, OHIO

PITTSBURGH, PENNSYLVANIA **COLUMBIA, SOUTH CAROLINA**

58 • CHAPTER THREE

SAN FRANCISCO, CALIFORNIA

ALBUQUERQUE, NEW MEXICO

SAN ANTONIO, TEXAS **AUSTIN, TEXAS**

Miami, Florida is an interesting case study in regards to the amount and quality of graffiti. Wynwood, a neighborhood north of downtown Miami, has an art district containing more than seventy galleries, museums and art collections. There is an ArtWalk once a month, and the neighborhood is home to Wynwood Walls, a permanent outdoor exhibit space featuring some of the world's best graffiti artists. All of this makes Wynwood one of the biggest street art districts in the world. Graffiti is a big part of Miami's culture and the designated area of Wynwood shows how the city celebrates this. With a few exceptions, I found that the graffiti in Miami isn't affected by the culture of the city as much as the culture of the city is affected by the graffiti. Storefronts consider it an honor to be tagged or have a mural painted on the side of the their building. Commissioned artwork is strategically placed and often is photographed or filmed as it is being created.

MIAMI, FLORIDA

This page is the work of a graffiti artist that goes by the name of RETNA. The picture to the right is another shot of that same piece of art. The picture below and the detailed shot to the right are also his work. He has a very distinct style that is a type of script derived from blackletter, Egyptian hieroglyphics, Arabic and Hebrew calligraphy that communicates poetry and personal messages.

Graffiti artists, like illustrators, are known for having a specific style that makes their work instantly recognizeable. It is within this repetition, no matter where their "canvas" is in the world, that they forge their own uniqe identity. Their style becomes their trademark and how they are known and celebrated. This ability to create an identity based on a style is certainly of interest to anyone interested in the serious study of typography.

MIAMI, FLORIDA

This spread is the work of Australian graffiti artist Rone. He started out decorating skateboards and skate parks and has become internationally known, with his work showing up in cities all over the world as well as galleries and exhibitions.

MIAMI, FLORIDA

> "I paint because I love it, and it adds character to any inanimate object. Whether it is a wall or a footpath. It brings the streets to life."
>
> — RONE

MIAMI, FLORIDA

Roa is a graffiti artist from Belgium that is known for painting animals that are native to the area of each painting. While not typography based, his artwork is very much influenced by the culture and his surroundings. His style is to use minimal colors while depicting animals in a realistic style. The painting below can be seen from several blocks away and it is simply breathtaking.

MIAMI, FLORIDA

MIAMI, FLORIDA

This is Fado (left), the main character found in the artwork of artist GG (Gabriel Gimenez). Below is the work of another artist found on telephone poles throughout Wynwood. These are great examples of how a signature style or character found in artwork make the graffiti artist identifiable.

GRAFFITI • 65

MIAMI, FLORIDA

MIAMI, FLORIDA

GRAFFITI

SEPARATED AT BIRTH

When looking back through pictures of my travels I often come across images that, while taken in different cities, convey a kinship or similarity. Sometimes the connection is obvious. The repetition of Shepard Fairey's OBEY image makes his work instantly recognizable. Other times the pairings are more intuitive like the images of playful children in bright clothes on the opposite page and the pattern based pairings on the following spread.

BOSTON, MASSACHUSETTS

AUSTIN, TEXAS

68 • CHAPTER THREE

SAN FRANCISCO, CALIFORNIA

BOSTON, MASSACHUSETTS

03 GRAFFITI

GRAFFITI • 69

AUSTIN, TEXAS

ALBUQUERQUE, NEW MEXICO

SYRACUSE, NEW YORK

70 • CHAPTER THREE

MIAMI, FLORIDA

SYRACUSE, NEW YORK

ALBUQUERQUE, NEW MEXICO

AKRON, OHIO

I first saw French graphic designer and typographer Massin's design for an edition of the play *The Bald Soprano* while I was in college. I fell in love with his black and white compositions and beautiful use of typography.

Massin's designs had a big effect on me during my formative years studying graphic design. I have so much respect for graffiti artists and their craft, as highlighted in this chapter, but there is something about stencil art that speaks to my heart the most. In most cases, it is obvious that the templated stencil that I come across is prepared in advance so the artist is able to "tag on the fly" while minimizing the risk of getting caught. It's also an easier way for an artist to brand themselves quickly throughout the city. I think my love for this style is a nod to the balance that Massin was able to capture in his work.

Massin has a way of showing just enough information without giving away all the details and yet being completely expressive at the same time. This is such a hard balance to achieve.

AUSTIN, TEXAS

MIAMI, FLORIDA

NEW HAVEN, CONNECTICUT

While murals are not considered graffiti per se, it made the most sense to group them in this chapter. The main difference between the two is that murals are commissioned artwork, graffiti is not. It is interesting to note that the murals I have come across *are* affected by the city they are located in. The colors, images and ideas that are utilized are directly inspired by the culture they reside in, which makes sense since the city has to approve the placement of the artwork.

ALBUQUERQUE, NEW MEXICO

MIAMI, FLORIDA   **ATLANTA, GEORGIA**

CLEVELAND, OHIO

NASHVILLE, TENNESSEE

SYRACUSE, NEW YORK

AUSTIN, TEXAS

BOSTON, MASSACHUSETTS

ALBUQUERQUE, NEW MEXICO

RICHMOND, VIRGINIA

This is one of the most interesting murals I have come across. The design interacts with the two walls of the alley and the parking structure that is across the street. Change where you stand by half a step and it throws off the entire perspecitve. A good lesson in perspective.

NEW HAVEN, CONNECTICUT

SAN FRANCISCO, CALIFORNIA

AUSTIN, TEXAS

CUYAHOGA FALLS, OHIO

COLUMBIA, SOUTH CAROLINA

CINCINNATI, OHIO

03 GRAFFITI

MIAMI, FLORIDA

80 • CHAPTER THREE

MIAMI, FLORIDA

I have to close out this chapter with what many consider to be "the holy grail" of graffiti: the work of Banksy. One of the most famous graffiti artists alive today, Banksy is known for his graffiti of political and social commentary on walls, bridges and streets around the world. I had the privilege of snapping this picture in the Little Havana neighborhood in Miami. You know you've made it when the city covers your graffiti with plexiglass to protect it instead of hiring a crew to paint over it.

“ Art should comfort the disturbed and disturb the comfortable."

— BANKSY

04 HAND-LETTERING

ATLANTA, GEORGIA

84 • CHAPTER FOUR

WHAT'S THE DIFFERENCE BETWEEN HAND LETTERING AND TYPOGRAPHY?

Hand Lettering is the drawing of letters or phrases. Typography is the entire system of letters that the user can put together in any combination.

You can find beautiful examples of hand lettering in virtually every city and with a greater abundance in cities where the general population isn't thriving economically. The picture on the opposite page is the outside of the Krog Street Tunnel, which links Cabbagetown and Inman Park neighborhoods. This tunnel is known for its constantly changing street art. Cabbagetown is located on Atlanta's east side and was founded in the late 1800's.

The lettering on the door and the illustrations were such a treat to discover. The dancing taco with his white gloves and cowboy boots combined with the Hand Lettering really convey an inviting feel and evoke the culture of the region.

SAN ANTONIO, TEXAS

Hand Lettering artists typically fall into one of two categories. First there are the artists who make an honest attempt to stay as close to the letterforms as humanly possible by either utilizing a stencil or possessing a ridiculously steady hand. For example, the picture below is the finish line for the Boston Marathon. This massive sign spans the width of the street. It is obvious this artist paid close attention to color, spacing, and craft with the letterforms. However, there is nothing in particular about the letters that is unique to Boston. On the other hand, there are the artists who let their personalities shine through the letterforms they are crafting, which can give the sign a life of its own. The artist who crafted Edgewood Tires on the opposite page, must have been influenced by flames, or angel wings. The creative elements added on to the E and T makes what could have been a straightforward hand lettered sign especially memorable. And just try to imagine this door in Cleveland (far right) set in Helvetica. The hand lettering offers a glimpse of the establishment's personality and it's approach to food. Similarly your typographic choices can convey so much about your own project's message. Studying hand lettering is a great way to find your next breakthrough idea.

BOSTON, MASSACHUSETTS

CLEVELAND, OHIO

ATLANTA, GEORGIA

BROOKLYN, NEW YORK

FREDERICKSBURG, VIRGINIA

GREER, SOUTH CAROLINA

NEW YORK CITY, NEW YORK

NASHVILLE, TENNESSEE

HUDSON, OHIO

MIAMI, FLORIDA

When artists inject an element of playfulness or an added detail within the letterforms of hand lettered type you can find some great sources of inspiration. This entrance sign in Cleveland (right) is especially memorable because of the flourish at the end of the word *Push*. Sure, one can make the case that the word *entrance* suffers from mega tight leading and forced uniform width, but I find all is right with the world when my eyes land on the perfect flow of the letters in *Push*, which ends with the graceful curl of the *h*. This a great example of how paying extra attention to detail can give your letterforms additional personality.

Here is a hand lettered sign found on a restaurant wall in Richmond. The p/arrow combination is such a great solution that probably would not have happened if this was set on a computer. That little arrow makes this such a memorable sign and a fantastic example of being creative with your letterforms.

RICHMOND, VIRGINIA

CLEVELAND, OHIO

AKRON, OHIO

04 HAND-LETTERING

BOSTON, MASSACHUSETTS

AKRON, OHIO

ATLANTA, GEORGIA

ALBUQUERQUE, NEW MEXICO

SIOUX FALLS, SOUTH DAKOTA

GREER, SOUTH CAROLINA

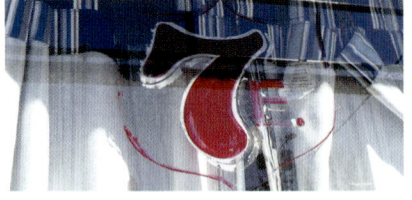

SAN ANTONIO, TEXAS

ORLANDO, FLORIDA

NASHVILLE, TENNESSEE

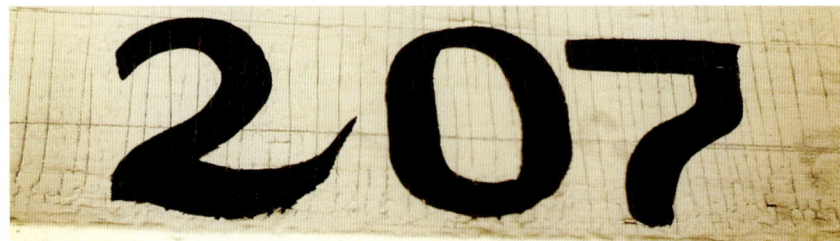

GREER, SOUTH CAROLINA

PITTSBURGH, PENNSYLVANIA

ALBUQUERQUE, NEW MEXICO

GREER, SOUTH CAROLINA

CUYAHOGA FALLS, OHIO   GREENVILLE, SOUTH CAROLINA

AUSTIN, TEXAS   CINCINNATI, OHIO

04 HAND-LETTERING

CINCINNATI, OHIO

NASHVILLE, TENNESSEE　　　**COLUMBIA, SOUTH CAROLINA**　　　**NEW YORK CITY, NEW YORK**

RICHMOND, VIRGINIA

> **QUICK TIP**
> Utilizing hand lettering requires you to plan ahead. See if you can spot the errors in these examples.

SAN ANTONIO, TEXAS

HAND-LETTERING • 97

RICHMOND, VIRGINIA

Right in the middle of downtown Richmond is this gem. This building dates back to the late 1800s as the Richmond Dairy Company. In 1999 the building was gutted to become apartments and luxury lofts now referred to as the Richmond Dairy Apartments. What makes this building unique is the three milk bottle structures on the corners. Of course not even giant milk bottles can distract attention from the beautiful black script lettering hanging on for dear life. Such a great fit for this building and what it once was. The carefree, flowing letters speak to the consistency of milk more than a stiff, structured serifed type would.

AKRON, OHIO

FREDERICKSBURG, VIRGINIA

COLUMBIA, SOUTH CAROLINA

MIAMI, FLORIDA

BOSTON, MASSACHUSETTS

I am continually amazed at the affect weather has on letterforms. It's interesting to observe how the letters start to fall apart. The beauty of weathering is undeniable. While probably not the preferred outcome for the business owner, it's a fun and inspiring design exercise to spot real weathering of letterforms on signs and compare with typefaces that try to mimic the effects. The lesson you'll likely learn is when trying to achieve an authentic distressed look in your work, do it the real way.

RICHMOND, VIRGINIA

CINCINNATI, OHIO

ATLANTA, GEORGIA

SAN ANTONIO, TEXAS

HAND-LETTERING

> "*A Love Letter to Syracuse* is a tribute. It is meant to be from Syracuse to Syracuse."
>
> — STEVE POWERS

I had an opportunity to study the work of Steve Powers during my trip to Syracuse. His series of lettering on bridges (also found in Brooklyn and Philadelphia) are affectionately referred to as love letters. He came up with the messages by spending time listening to locals talk about their hometown. "Now That We Are Here, Nowhere Else Matters" speaks to hope and "Spring Comes, Summer Waits, Fall Leaves, Winter Longs" celebrates the intense seasons of Syracuse. He strategically targets "rust belt" areas in the hopes of transforming the neighborhoods. It is important to note that this is not graffiti, it is commissioned artwork by the City of Syracuse.

SYRACUSE, NEW YORK

SYRACUSE, NEW YORK

Austin, Texas is one of the cities most affected by culture in terms of hand lettering, in my opinion. San Antonio may have more in terms of sheer volume and Boston's handlettering may prove to be the most sophisticated, but Austin exemplifies the slogan "go big or go home." The size and quality of the hand lettered signs there are like nothing I've ever seen before. A fantastic example of this is Frank, a restaurant with a gigantic bold hand lettered sign (below, bottom.) Plus, the side of the building is designated for public art (below, top.) This is reminiscent of the public art concept of the aforementioned Wynwood walls in Miami, though the artwork is very different.

AUSTIN, TEXAS

As I was walking on South Congress (SoCo shopping district) in Austin, Texas, I came across TOMS. This is the second free standing TOMS shoe store in the United States and had just opened a couple weeks before I was there. The renovated Victorian house is beautiful, but what really caught my eye was the lettering on the side of the building that speaks to the premise of the company: TOMS will match every pair of shoes purchased with a pair of new shoes to a child in need. The design and four letters, while shocking to see in contrast with the Victorian design of the building, totally fit into the culture of the city—and clearly communicates the mission of TOMS.

AUSTIN, TEXAS

AUSTIN, TEXAS

AUSTIN, TEXAS

HAND-LETTERING

05 SIGNAGE

NASHVILLE, TENNESSEE

RICHMOND, VIRGINIA

SIOUX FALLS, SOUTH DAKOTA

ORLANDO, FLORIDA

112 • CHAPTER FIVE

Out of all of the chapters in this book, this chapter is the most far reaching. Neon signs, hand lettered signs, ghost signs and wayfinding signs are all kinds of signage, but in order to compare how they are handled from city to city, they are best covered in their own chapter. The images for this chapter are organized based on the kinds of business that is being advertised. It is interesting to see how the culture of the city has played a part in decisions that have been made for the typography, the material for the sign (metal, wood, concrete, and so forth), and the colors utilized. I find the signs in this chapter to be a big source of inspiration because they offer creativity in very structured environments—especially the signs that advertise locally owned businesses. There are size requirements that have to be taken into account, color combinations that have to be thought through, and most importantly, the sign has to be memorable.

QUICK TIP

Check out different points of view. When a sign really catches my attention, I take several pictures of it. One from a distance for scale and surroundings and then several zooming in on the details that make it unique. Or, in the case of Macy's (below), three signs on one building handled three different ways!

NEW YORK CITY, NEW YORK

ALBUQUERQUE, NEW MEXICO

COLUMBUS, OHIO

CLEVELAND, OHIO

NEW YORK CITY, NEW YORK

SAN FRANCISCO, CALIFORNIA

MIAMI, FLORIDA

AUSTIN, TEXAS

COLUMBIA, SOUTH CAROLINA

ALBUQUERQUE, NEW MEXICO

I have found one of the hardest things to accomplish as a designer is successfully pairing different typefaces, especially when a script is involved. The signs on this spread offer creative solutions using varying sizes and colors to help set the tone for the business.

CLEVELAND, OHIO

AKRON, OHIO

BOSTON, MASSACHUSETTS

RICHMOND, VIRGINIA

SIOUX FALLS, SOUTH DAKOTA

NASHVILLE, TENNESSEE

COLUMBIA, SOUTH CAROLINA

> **"** Creativity involves breaking out of established patterns in order to look at things in a different way."
>
> — EDWARD DE BONO

COLUMBUS, OHIO **SAN ANTONIO, TEXAS** **ATLANTA, GEORGIA**

NEW YORK CITY, NEW YORK

NEW YORK CITY, NEW YORK

BOSTON, MASSACHUSETTS

MIAMI, FLORIDA

SIOUX FALLS, SOUTH DAKOTA

05 SIGNAGE

SIGNAGE • 119

PITTSBURGH, PENNSYLVANIA

SIOUX FALLS, SOUTH DAKOTA

CINCINNATI, OHIO

ORLANDO, FLORIDA

AKRON, OHIO

The Niagara Mohawk Building houses the Niagara Mohawk power utility company. It is a classic example of art deco architecture and was added to the National Register of Historic Places in 2010. According to the National Park Service:

"The Niagara Hudson Building is an outstanding example of Art Deco architecture and a symbol of the Age of Electricity. Completed in 1932, the building became the headquarters for the nation's largest electric utility company and expressed the technology of electricity through its modernistic design, material, and extraordinary program of exterior lighting. The design elements applied by architects Melvin L. King and Bley & Lyman transformed a corporate office tower into a widely admired beacon of light and belief in the future. With its central tower and figurative winged sculpture personifying electric lighting, nicknamed Iron Mike, the powerfully sculpted and decorated building offered a symbol of optimism and progress in the context of the Great Depression."

This is one of those buildings that will take your breath away. The level of detail is amazing to see and it's interesting to note that a lot of the materials used to build the structure came from local resources.

SYRACUSE, NEW YORK

MIAMI, FLORIDA

NEW YORK CITY, NEW YORK

PENINSULA, OHIO

BOSTON, MASSACHUSETTS

AUSTIN, TEXAS

SAN FRANCISCO, CALIFORNIA

ALBUQUERQUE, NEW MEXICO

PITTSBURGH, PENNSYLVANIA

This pictures here showcase examples of double rail mounted signs. These types of signs, which are getting harder to come by, really highlight each letter. They are like a crown, perched at the top of the building, creating a regal effect.

SIOUX FALLS, SOUTH DAKOTA

PITTSBURGH, PENNSYLVANIA

NEW YORK CITY, NEW YORK

CLEVELAND, OHIO

RICHMOND, VIRGINIA

Orpheum Theaters: San Francisco's landmark Orpheum Theater first opened in 1926. Its unique facade was based on a twelfth century French cathedral. The interior features vaulted ceilings and seats 2,203 guests. In 1998 the theater was completely renovated; $20 million was spent to make the Orpheum suitable for Broadway shows. Orpheum Theatre in Sioux Falls opened in 1913 as a vaudeville house and seats approximately 700 occupants. This elegant theater became a B-movie theater in 1927 and was later aquired by the Community Playhouse group in 1954 who used the space until 2002. Today it is owned by the City of Sioux Falls and hosts concerts, plays and community events. The Sioux Falls Orpheum Theater was added to the National Register of Historic Places in 1983.

Byrd Theater: One of the nation's grand movie palaces, the Byrd Theater of Richmond, Virginia was built in 1928 and is considered both a State and National Historic Landmark. Named after William Byrd II, one of the founders of Richmond, the Byrd Theater has remained largely unchanged since it opened. The venue continues to show movies to this day and remains one of the nation's cinematic treasures.

SAN FRANCISCO, CALIFORNIA

SIOUX FALLS, SOUTH DAKOTA

Fillmore Theater Miami Beach: Originally called the Miami Beach Auditorium, this theater was built in 1957. In 2007, it was renovated and was renamed The Fillmore as an expansion of the famous brand started by The Fillmore in San Francisco.

Lincoln Theater: Built in 1936, the Lincoln Theatre of Miami Beach was a movie theater and later a concert hall designed in the art deco style. It functioned as a cinema until the 1980s, then sat vacant for several years before becoming retail space.

Ace Theater: Built in 1925, the Ace Theatre served African-American moviegoers in the Coconut Grove community during segregation. It operated as a movie theater into the late 1970s and was later used for church services and community events.

Cleveland Public Theater: Founded in 1981, CPT is Cleveland's premier stage for adventurous new theatre. The theater is nationally recognized for its ground breaking work. It is listed on the National Register of Historic Places.

MIAMI, FLORIDA

CLEVELAND, OHIO

I refer to the examples on this spread as "industrial typography." These are little finds that are usually smaller than one's hand and are typically in hidden spots. For example, King (opposite page, top left) was found on the bottom of a concrete slab that holds a lamp post. I had to lay on my stomach in order to take the photo because the logo was so tiny. But I found it amazing to see such a well designed logo in such an obscure place. It's proof that well designed typography can be found anywhere; you just have to be on the look out!

For example, train tracks are another great place to find well designed type (in addition to killer graffiti). Case in point: the General Railway Signal logo (opposite page, far right). These three letters look like they have always been intertwined with each other and is such a strong solution compared to typical monogrammed letters that are often seen on the backs of cars or embroidered on clothes.

GREENVILLE, SOUTH CAROLINA

CINCINNATI, OHIO **NEW YORK CITY, NEW YORK** **GREER, SOUTH CAROLINA**

FREDERICKSBURG, VIRGINIA

SYRACUSE, NEW YORK

SAN ANTONIO, TEXAS

CLEVELAND, OHIO

Originally designed in the Chicago style, the Scarbrough Building is Austin's first skyscraper. Built between 1908 and 1909, it was among the most modern buildings at the time. In the 1930s, the building underwent renovations and the exterior was redesigned in the art deco style. Today, only the cornice and upper floor windows reveal the Scarbrough Building's Chicago style origins.

AUSTIN, TEXAS

MIAMI, FLORIDA

CUYAHOGA FALLS, OHIO

One of the most valuable things I've learned in my travels is about what makes a sign successful. Going from city to city, there are a few constant design elements that are important regardless of location. First, the right typeface needs to be chosen for the business that's being advertised. It's always a good idea when selecting a typeface to do some research to see what other companies have used it and in what capacity. Colors, kerning and leading also play a very important role. Of course, the most important element when designing a sign is to make it memorable. I was in Sioux Falls, South Dakota for three days and this funeral home sign (below) is the sign that I remember most from my time there. The stark red three dimensional letters on the white background really pop in the neutral colored environment. The contrasting typefaces is a good choice and the spacing is generous which is easy on the eyes. The signage has flaws—notice the spacing between "funeral" and "home"—but it is memorable. Illustrations in signage are another way to create a lasting impression. I took the Safety Shoes picture in Boston (opposite page, top left) more than ten years ago and it is still my favorite illustrated sign. It was attached to the side of a ship in the Boston Harbor. The colors are totally fitting in the environment and the composition creates a lasting impression.

SIOUX FALLS, SOUTH DAKOTA

132 • CHAPTER FIVE

BOSTON, MASSACHUSETTS

NASHVILLE, TENNESSEE **ORLANDO, FLORIDA** **SAN ANTONIO, TEXAS**

NEW YORK CITY, NEW YORK **ALBUQUERQUE, NEW MEXICO** **COLUMBIA, SOUTH CAROLINA**

05 SIGNAGE

This spread highlights some jewelery store signs. The plaque taken at the entrance of the store in Richmond (below left) is one of the most detailed signs I have ever come across. This three dimensional sign reminded me of a letterpressing. The level of detail that is contained in such a small area (about the size of one's hand) is just amazing. I can only imagine what the jewelery inside looks like!

In stark contrast is the three dimensional sign taken in San Francisco (right and opposite page). It's poorly kerned letters set on concrete that is falling apart. (Plus, the letters were covered with bird poop.)

SAN FRANCISCO, CALIFORNIA

RICHMOND, VIRGINIA

FREDERICKSBURG, VIRGINIA

SAN FRANCISCO, CALIFORNIA

AKRON, OHIO

RICHMOND, VIRGINIA

BOSTON, MASSACHUSETTS

MIAMI, FLORIDA

CINCINNATI, OHIO

SYRACUSE, NEW YORK

CHARLESTON, SOUTH CAROLINA

PITTSBURGH, PENNSYLVANIA

NEW YORK CITY, NEW YORK

SAN ANTONIO, TEXAS

05 SIGNAGE

SIGNAGE • 139

06 NEON SIGNS

Neon signs were introduced at a demonstration in December 1910 by Georges Claude at the Paris Motor Show. These electric signs are lit by tubes containing rarefied neon or other gases. Neon signs were popular in the United States from the 1920s to the 1960s, but have since seen a decline. Many cities are now finding themselves trying to preserve and restore vintage neon signs.

MIAMI, FLORIDA

MIAMI, FLORIDA

> **QUICK TIP**
>
> The next time you are close to a neon sign, it's worth the time to stop and really look at how the neon bends and contorts to fit within the letterforms—or even better, how the neon itself makes up the letterforms. If you find that the sign is double-sided, take a good look at both sides. Since neon signs are built by hand, each side is unique!

NEON SIGNS • 143

Despite their decline, you'll find neon signs in pretty much any city you visit—both old signs and new ones. In this chapter I've grouped them by the kinds of businesses they advertise and two things became apparent: (1) hotels and restaurants utilize neon signs more than any other business, and (2) Miami loves neon. It's everywhere.

FREDERICKSBURG, VIRGINAI

SAN ANTONIO, TEXAS

MIAMI, FLORIDA

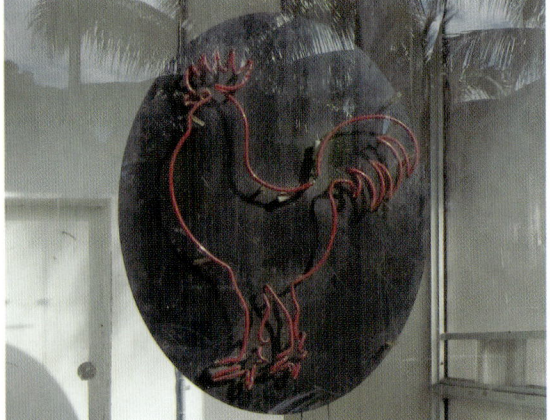

NEW YORK CITY, NEW YORK

144 • CHAPTER SIX

SAN FRANCISCO, CALIFORNIA

AKRON, OHIO

SIOUX FALLS, SOUTH DAKOTA

FREDERICKSBURG, VIRGINIA

While this chapter focuses on neon signs, I have also included signs that feature lightbulbs. The Empress sign (right) is a great example of a sign that features both types of lighting. Signs utilizing lightbulbs don't seem to be as common as neon signs. Most likely because light bulbs require more maintaince and don't last as long as neon signs—but the lightbulbs do give the signs a nice nostalgic feel.

On the opposite page is a jewelery store in Austin that was established in 1906. Walking by a store with this kind of signage you can't help but feel nostalgic and think "they don't make them like this anymore." The store uses several styles of signs and each one is unique while maintaining consistency with the branding. For example, the strokes of the letterfroms in the sign built into the floor are thinner than the neon sign letters but the overall style is consistent.

SAN FRANCISCO, CALIFORNIA

AUSTIN, TEXAS

ALBUQUERQUE, NEW MEXICO

AUSTIN, TEXAS

MIAMI, FLORIDA

148 • CHAPTER SIX

SIOUX FALLS, SOUTH DAKOTA

AUSTIN, TEXAS

SAN FRANCISCO, CALIFORNIA

SAN ANTONIO, TEXAS

CUYAHOGA FALLS, OHIO

CINCINNATI, OHIO

150 • CHAPTER SIX

RICHMOND, VIRGINIA

AUSTIN, TEXAS

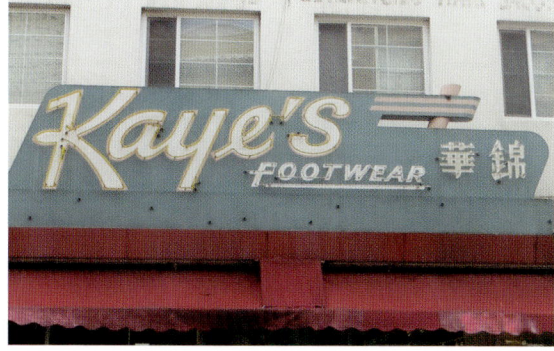

SAN FRANCISCO, CALIFORNIA

PITTSBURGH, PENNSYLVANIA

NASHVILLE, TENNESSEE

NEON SIGNS

Theater signs and marquees are a great place to find examples of lighted signage. I love researching theaters signs, marquees and even the architecture of the buildings where historic theaters are found. Typically, there is great detail that goes into the design of a theater, and the architecture and signage is often a direct reflection of the city. Most of the old theaters that I have come across are not only considered landmarks of the city, they are also on the National Register of Historic Places—an official list of the Nation's historic places worthy of preservation.

The following pages showcase some great examples of lighted theater signs. It is interesting to note the year that each theater was built and how the signs and architecture style vary from city to city.

The Ohio Theatre marquee (below, left) perfectly fits in downtown Cleveland. The structural slab serif typeface and the black and silver color scheme speaks to the steel mill city. The Paramount marquee (opposite page, far right) is a perfect fit for Boston. It's interesting to compare the KiMo Theater in Albuquerque and the Aztec Theater in San Antonio on the next pages. All three theaters were built a year apart from each other and yet look completely different. They all have such unique characteristics that tie specifically to the city they are located in. The culture of the city has affected every design choice that was made.

CLEVELAND, OHIO

SAN FRANCISCO, CALIFORNIA

AKRON, OHIO

SIOUX FALLS, SOUTH DAKOTA

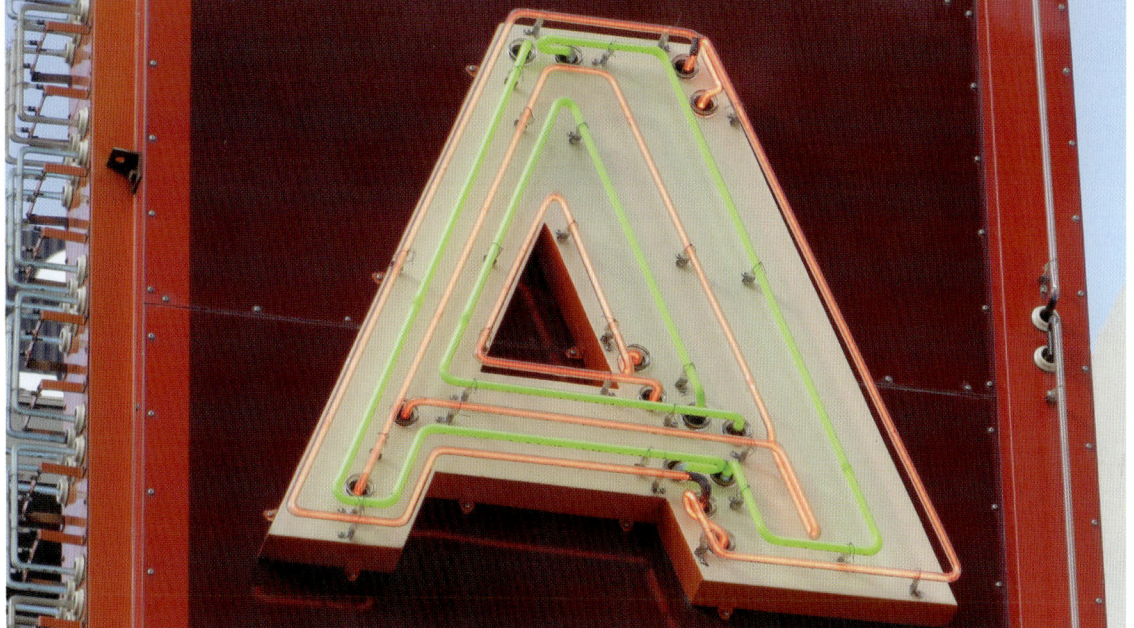

AUSTIN, TEXAS

BOSTON, MASSACHUSETTS

> "The future of architecture is culture."
> — PHILIP JOHNSON

ALBUQUERQUE, NEW MEXICO

PITTSBURGH, PENNSYLVANIA

CHARLESTON, SOUTH CAROLINA

PITTSBURGH, PENNSYLVANIA

SAN ANTONIO, TEXAS

NEON SIGNS

Restaurants seem to utilize neon signs for getting customers in the door more than any other type of business. Looking for breakfast, lunch or dinner? A diner, bakery or coffee shop? Neon signs light the way. The most common type treatment for the lettering is all caps sans serif. This is surprising given the way the neon tubes attach to each other. You might expect to find more script and connectivity with the letterforms.

AKRON, OHIO

AKRON, OHIO

NEW YORK CITY, NEW YORK

AUSTIN, TEXAS

AUSTIN, TEXAS

FREDERICKSBURG, VIRGINIA

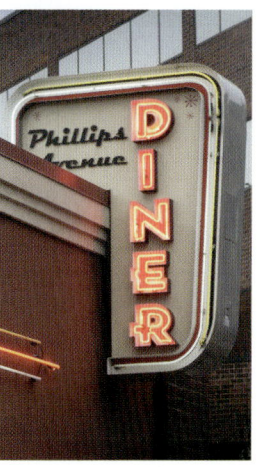

CUYAHOGA FALLS, OHIO

SIOUX FALLS, SOUTH DAKOTA

06 NEON SIGNS

NEON SIGNS • 157

BOSTON, MASSACHUSETTS

158 • CHAPTER SIX

BOSTON, MASSACHUSETTS   **NEW HAVEN, CONNECTICUT**

ATLANTA, GEORGIA   **AUSTIN, TEXAS**   **RICHMOND, VIRGINIA**

NEON SIGNS

SAN ANTONIO, TEXAS

BOSTON, MASSACHUSETTS

BOSTON, MASSACHUSETTS

SAN FRANCISCO, CALIFORNIA

AUSTIN, TEXAS

BOSTON, MASSACHUSETTS

SIOUX FALLS, SOUTH DAKOTA **NEW HAVEN, CONNECTICUT** **AUSTIN, TEXAS**

CLEVELAND, OHIO **SAN ANTONIO, TEXAS** **PENINSULA, OHIO**

SAN FRANCISCO, CALIFORNIA

ATLANTA, GEORGIA

AKRON, OHIO

SAN ANTONIO, TEXAS

BOSTON, MASSACHUSETTS

AUSTIN, TEXAS

NEON SIGNS • 163

CINCINNATI, OHIO

SAN FRANCISCO, CALIFORNIA

NASHVILLE, TENNESSEE

PITTSBURGH, PENNSYLVANIA

AUSTIN, TEXAS

AKRON, OHIO

COLUMBUS, OHIO

SAN ANTONIO, TEXAS

COLUMBUS, OHIO

CUYAHOGA FALLS, OHIO

Neon signs are a big part of the look of any city. The presence of neon signs seems to evoke the feeling of bustle and a thriving night life. While you may not always find that the signs influenced by the culture of the city, you can't deny that neon signs contribute to each city's personality.

PITTSBURGH, PENNSYLVANIA

CLEVELAND, OHIO

NASHVILLE, TENNESSEE

MIAMI, FLORIDA

SALEM, OHIO

AKRON, OHIO

NEON SIGNS

07 WAYFINDING

Wayfinding is a term used in the context of architecture to describe the user experience of orienting oneself and navigating one's environment. It also refers to architectural or design elements that aid orientation. Urban planner Kevin A. Lynch, author of the book *The Image of the City*, defined wayfinding as "a consistent use and organization of definite sensory cues from the external environment."

Wayfinding signs are interesting in the context of culture because while there is definitely a standard look that can be found across the country, there are pockets in each city where the local culture has staked its claim and influenced the design choices.

ALBUQUERQUE, NEW MEXICO

CLEVELAND, OHIO

NEW YORK CITY, NEW YORK

QUICK TIP

Any sign that points you in the direction of where you need to go qualifies as a wayfinding sign: street signs, parking signs, numbers on buildings and directional signs. If it helps you get to where you are going, it's wayfinding!

AUSTIN, TEXAS

07 WAYFINDING

Parking signs seem to be designed with more permanence than many other kinds of signs. The materials that are chosen and the structures that are put in place to hold the signs or individual letters are meant to be there for a very long time. There is less risk taken in regards to the typefaces that are chosen and the placement of the letters. The images on the following spreads include a few of the more interesting signs that I have come across in my travels. Typically, parking signs are large, bold, and usually created in san serif type that often times lacks color. Signs that take a different approach, whether in the way the sign is mounted or the way the neon is being used, are refreshing and offer a good lesson in the visual power of the unexpected.

Most cities take a standard approach to wayfinding but what I did find are little pockets within each city that buck the system. Some areas do their own thing in a way specific to the culture of the city and the result can be quite memorable. Albuquerque is a great example of successfully doing the unexpected. You'll see examples of their wayfinding sprinkled throughout this chapter.

> " I don't think that type should be expressive at all. I can write the word *dog* with any typeface and it doesn't have to look like a dog. But there are people that think that when they write *dog* it should bark."
>
> — MASSIMO VIGNELLI

CHARLESTON, SOUTH CAROLINA

NASHVILLE, TENNESSEE

PENINSULA, OHIO

NEW YORK CITY, NEW YORK

NEW HAVEN, CONNECTICUT

ALBUQUERQUE, NEW MEXICO

SAN FRANCISCO, CALIFORNIA

ALBUQUERQUE, NEW MEXICO

MIAMI, FLORIDA

NEW HAVEN, CONNECTICUT

SYRACUSE, NEW YORK

07 WAYFINDING

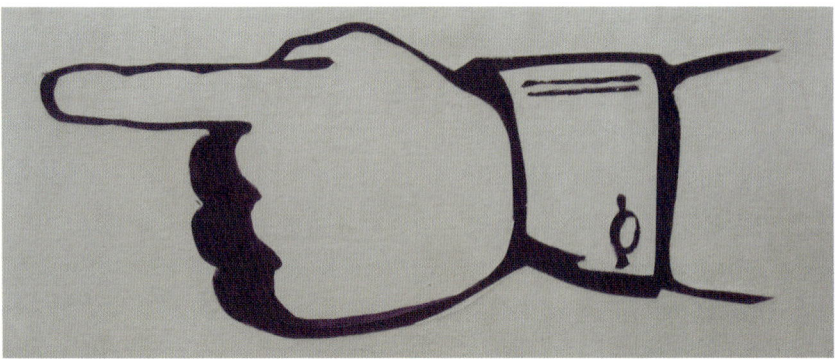

BOSTON, MASSACHUSETTS

CINCINNATI, OHIO

The next few images showcase wayfinding signs that literally point you in the direction that you need to go. From the conservative arrow leading the way to the surprising manicule (the pointing finger symbol commonly used in printing), these images represent some different takes on wayfinding. With wayfinding, visual cues are just as important (if not more) than the words themselves.

SYRACUSE, NEW YORK

SAN ANTONIO, TEXAS

CLEVELAND, OHIO

GREER, SOUTH CAROLINA

The pictures on these two pages are specific to way-finding transportation. These types of signs are typically unique to the city they are located in. The sign in the Nob Hill area of Albuquerque (below) advertises a bus stop that takes you to (or from) the Alvarado Transportation Center (right). This building is illustrated on the sign. You won't find that sign in any other city in the world. San Francisco is known for their cable cars as a means of transportation so it's only fitting that these signs adorn the city streets (below right). The sign taken in Miami (opposite page, far right) letting people know that the surface is about to change (from asphalt to sand) is another example of signs that are specific to their location. You won't find a sign like that in a land locked state.

ALBUQUERQUE, NEW MEXICO

ALBUQUERQUE, NEW MEXICO

SAN FRANCISCO, CALIFORNIA

NEW YORK CITY, NEW YORK

MIAMI, FLORIDA

NASHVILLE, TENNESSEE

Since I'm always on the lookout for unique signs that catch my eye, you can imagine my surprise when I came across these two property lines while walking around downtown San Antonio (below left). After doing some research, I found out that Joske's was a department store that was founded in 1867 by a German immigrant named Julian Joske. In late 1920s Hahn Department Stores acquired Joske's along with some other department stores in dalls, and a few years later the company became part of Allied Stores. In the 1980s Allied was taken over by Campeau and the Joske's chain was sold to Dillard's. At that point the Joske's stores were converted into Dillard's locations.

There must have been a feud between Joske and someone to merit this plaque. It's funny to note that there isn't an apostrophe—but there is a period. I rounded the corner and came across the property line plaque below it, which looks to have been done at at a different point in time. The arrows and the tightly kerned letters look modest but at close inspection a very different tone emerges. I'm especially drawn to the arrows breaking the border to point exactly to where the property line is. That little detail gives this plaque the extra punch needed to really drive the message home.

These two private property signs found in Boston (below right) were also found within yards of each other in the middle of a sidewalk. Since there is no name attached to either of them, I am unable to research the history so I can only assume another heated battle over property led to the placement of these two signs.

SAN ANTONIO, TEXAS

BOSTON, MASSACHUSETTS

PITTSBURGH, PENNSYLVANIA

AUSTIN, TEXAS

SAN FRANCISCO, CALIFORNIA

One of the first lessons I learned when I started researching vernacular typography is that there are different requirements that need to be considered than for typefaces selected for hand-held printed work. If you think about driving by in a car and trying to read the numbers on a building to get where you are going, they need to be legible in less than two seconds. An elaborate script typeface will not work. An embellished script is suitable for wedding invitations or something meant to be held in your hand and studied over time. But for quick reading, a typeface that is sans serif, bold and set with generous spacing is the most successful. The larger the typeface the more liberties can be taken. These liberties can include super tight kerning, uniquely placed 3-D numbers, or, my personal favorite, numbers that look like they are jumping off the top of the building as in the picture on the bottom far right taken in Albuquerque. How's that for memorable?!

CLEVELAND, OHIO

COLUMBIA, SOUTH CAROLINA

BOSTON, MASSACHUSETTS

SAN FRANCISCO, CALIFORNIA

ALBUQUERQUE, NM

CUYAHOGA FALLS, OHIO   **AUSTIN, TEXAS**

NEW YORK CITY, NEW YORK   **SAN ANTONIO, TEXAS**   **BOSTON, MASSACHUSETTS**

07 WAYFINDING

The address on the building in Pittsburgh (below, left) is the largest I've come across. This is a great example of taking an address, something that most people overlook, and turning it into a memorable design element. The way the letters are formed reminds me of bent paperclips. A few months after snapping this picture, I was in Cincinnati and visited the American Sign Museum. You can imagine my surprise when I came across the 200 main street sign, I asked the owner of the museum about this sign and he confessed that he had hired a man from Pittsburgh to model this storefront to look like a building in Pittsburgh. Beautiful!

GREENVILLE, SOUTH CAROLINA

MIAMI, FLORIDA

SAN ANTONIO, TEXAS

SAN FRANCISCO, CALIFORNIA

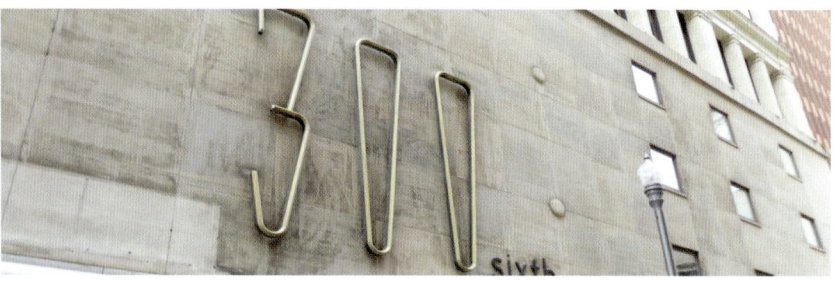

PITTSBURGH, PENNSYLVANIA

CINCINNATI, OHIO

When text is set in all capital letters, it is not as legible. Readers find themselves at a disadvantage because they don't have the visual cues that make words quickly recognizable that they have with lowercase text. According to *Typographic Design: Form and Communication* by Rob Carter, Philip B. Meggs, Ben Day, Sandra Maxa and Mark Sanders, "The irregular word shape, ascenders, and descenders provide rich contrasts that assure satisfactory perception." Spacing of letterforms is another factor that can disrupt the the legibility of words.

It's interesting to note the amount of street signs out there that buck the system (either on purpose or out of ignorance) and make a go of poorly set type.

AUSTIN, TEXAS

CHARLESTON, SOUTH CAROLINA

NEW YORK CITY, NEW YORK

SAN FRANCISCO, CALIFORNIA

CINCINNATI, OHIO

Is there a way to create wayfinding signs that are not only functional, but also well designed? Of course there is! The examples on this spread are functional wayfinding signs that serve a purpose but are creative and pleasing to the eye at the same time. Would you rather lock your bike to a boring metal bike rack or one of these pictured below?

Street banners (opposite page) can usually be found attached to lamp posts lining streets advertising an upcoming event or just welcoming you to the city. These are usually a playful blend of typography and illustrations.

SYRACUSE, NEW YORK

CLEVELAND, OHIO

MIAMI, FLORIDA

SYRACUSE, NEW YORK

SIOUX FALLS, SOUTH DAKOTA

SAN FRANCISCO, CALIFORNIA

07 WAYFINDING

WAYFINDING • 189

08 CULTURAL OBSERVATIONS

In my research for my design presentations in various cities, I noticed a theme starting to emerge. The theme of what truly identifies a city's culture started to take shape with pictures that were sent in to me from local creatives but then reinforced when I visited the cities in person. Orlando and San Antonio are a couple of good examples. For Orlando, I was expecting to receive a lot of pictures from Disney World that featured the famous theme park. Instead, I received an overwhelming number of pictures that celebrated the City of Orlando, the Orlando Museum of Art, and the Orlando Public Library, just to name a few. The residents identified more with what made the city unique, rather than the tourist destination that the city is so known for around the world.

For San Antonio, I was convinced that I'd be bombarded with pictures from The Alamo. It is conveniently located in the downtown area, it is free and open to the public, and it is a definite must-see for anyone visiting the city. To my surprise, I didn't receive one picture. As I found out, it is the destination for countless fieldtrips, the suggested topic for history papers, and you can't turn a corner in the city and not see a business that uses "Alamo" somewhere in their name. It's Alamo overload and most locals don't identify with it at all. They've become numb to having the Alamo located in the heart of their city. What did emerge from the pictures I received was an abundance of hand lettering. While this is in part due to the economic status of the business owners, the results make for a very unique typographic landscape.

ORLANDO, FLORIDA

SAN ANTONIO, TEXAS

While my findings from Orlando and San Antonio took me by surprise, the results from Miami and Cleveland were a bit more expected. The citizens of Miami celebrated their beautiful neon signs and the amazing graffiti that is on display throughout the city.

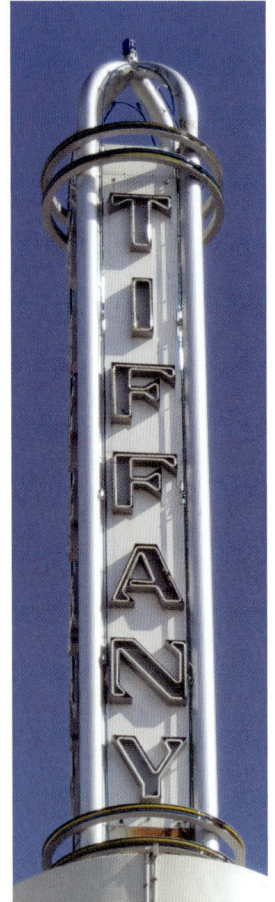

MIAMI, FLORIDA

MIAMI, FLORIDA

08
CULTURAL OBSERVATIONS

Stainless steel typography proved to be the dominant theme in Cleveland. Most likely a nod to the steel mill history of the city. While this isn't a surprise, it was shocking that no one sent in pictures of the typographic signs on the stadiums of the Cleveland Indians, Cleveland Cavaliers or the Cleveland Browns. Cleveland is such a sports town and even though the teams have been struggling with success, they are very much part of the identity of the city.

CLEVELAND, OHIO

The saying goes, Get your kicks on Route 66. I got my kicks all right! Visiting Albuquerque proved to be such a rewarding experience for letterhunting. The famous Route 66 that cuts through the city is populated with vintage signs that are still in remarkable condition. The Aztec Motel, built in 1932, was demolished in 2011 but the sign (below, center) has been preserved and will be incorporated into future development. There is an abundance of hotels and motels that are so unique and with varying typographic styles.

ALBUQUERQUE, NEW MEXICO

CULTURAL OBSERVATIONS • 197

I quickly learned that Yale University essentially makes up New Haven, Connecticut. While walking around the campus the day after my speaking engagement, I noticed that a lot of the buildings had this very specific type treatment on the buildings, usually around doors or above entryways. It seems to be a cross between black letter and script. This unusual hybrid makes for very interesting letterforms that, while difficult to read, are unique to this area. I've come across similar lettering before in different cities that I have visited (usually on graves), but never to this degree.

NEW HAVEN, CONNECTICUT

The color pallete of the typographic landscape in Miami would best be described as being neon bright. Albuquerque utilized a more Navajo color scheme throughout the city and New Haven rocked the concrete. What struck me about Sioux Falls was the lack of color. As a visitor seeing the city for the first time, I felt like the signs had been soaked in muted earth tones. While the city came across as being very modest and understated, I found it interesting that the Convention Center & Visitors Bureau not only utilizes a giant exclamation point, but the puncuation mark is pulling double duty by standing in for the "I". I thought this was a pretty bold move for this city!

SIOUX FALLS, SOUTH DAKOTA

CULTURAL OBSERVATIONS • 199

If you were a visitor in the city you live in, how would you see it differently?

I hope this book encourages you to look at your surroundings in a new way and to notice how unique each city is. One of the reasons traveling is such a rewarding experience for most people is that you are thrust out of your enviornment and dropped into a new one where all of your senses are awakened. From eating different meals in unique restaurants, to experiencing sights and sounds in new surroundings, you are taking in what the city has to offer. If you can get to a place where you are in that state of awareness in your day to day life, in the city you live in, you will be more mindful of your surroundings.

SYRACUSE, NEW YORK **GREER, SOUTH CAROLINA** **NEW YORK CITY, NEW YORK** **SAN FRANCISCO, CALIFORNIA** **RICHMOND, VIRGINIA** **AKRON, OHIO**

AUTHOR NIKKI VILLAGOMEZ PHOTOGRAPHED BY MARGARET GONZALEZ

MIAMI, FLORIDA

Index

Ace Theater (Miami, FL), 125
Akron, Ohio
    hand-lettered signs, 91, 92, 100
    manhole covers, 48, 53
    miscellaneous signs, 15, 117, 120, 136
    neon signs, 145, 152, 156, 163, 165, 169, 200
    Urban Art/graffiti, 71
Albuquerque, New Mexico, 33, 152, 154, 197, 197
    hand-lettered signs, 92, 94
    manhole covers and storm drain plaques, 39, 42, 43, 45, 47, 51
    miscellaneous signs, 22, 111, 114, 116, 122, 133, 197
    neon signs, 146, 152, 154
    Urban Art/graffiti and murals, 59, 70, 71, 74, 76
    wayfinding signs, 172, 176, 177, 180, 184, 191
apostrophes, signs and, 12, 16, 29
Art Deco buildings, 32, 34, 121, 125, 130
Atlanta, Georgia, 2, 33
    hand-lettered signs, 84-85, 87, 92, 103
    manhole covers, 50, 53
    miscellaneous signs, 15, 23, 118
    mural, 74
    neon signs, 159, 163
Austin, Texas, 2, 130
    hand-lettered signs, 95, 106-109
    manhole covers and storm drain plaques, 40, 42, 43, 44, 45, 46, 48
    miscellaneous signs, 11, 28, 116, 122
    neon signs, 146, 147, 149, 151, 153, 156, 157, 159, 160, 162, 163, 164
    Urban Art/graffiti and mural, 59, 68, 70, 72, 76, 79
    wayfinding signs, 173, 183, 185, 187
Aztec Motel (Albuquerque, NM), 197
Aztec Theater (San Antonio, TX), 152, 155

Banksy, 81
Boston, Massachusetts, 12, 13, 152, 153
    hand-lettered signs, 86, 92, 101, 106
    manhole covers and storm drain plaque, 40, 43, 44, 48, 51, 52
    miscellaneous signs, 12, 13, 15, 117, 119, 122, 132, 133, 136
    neon signs, 152, 153, 158, 159, 160, 161, 163
    Urban Art/graffiti and mural, 68, 69, 76
    wayfinding signs, 178, 182, 184, 185
Brooklyn, New York, 88
Byrd Theater (Richmond, VA), 124

Charleston, South Carolina
    miscellaneous signs, 31, 138
    neon sign, 154
    wayfinding signs, 174, 187
Chicago Style architecture, 130
Cincinnati, Ohio, 2, 16
    hand-lettered signs, 95, 96, 103
    industrial typography, 126, 127
    miscellaneous, 11, 16, 25, 26, 28, 30, 120, 138
    neon signs, 150, 164
    Urban Art/graffiti, 79

    wayfinding signs, 178, 186, 187
Cincinnati Color Building, 16
Claude, Georges, 142
Cleveland, Ohio, 2, 125, 152, 194, 196
    hand-lettered signs, 86, 87, 90
    industrial typography, 126, 127
    manhole covers, 38, 40
    miscellaneous signs, 10, 15, 22, 24, 26, 115, 117, 123, 129, 196
    neon signs, 152, 162, 168
    Urban Art/graffiti and murals, 58, 75
    wayfinding signs, 173, 179, 184, 188
Cleveland Public Theater (Cleveland, OH), 125
color, 16, 86, 117, 132
    local culture and, 1, 74, 113, 132, 152, 200
Columbia, South Carolina, 1, 2
    hand-lettered signs, 96, 100
    miscellaneous signs, 20, 25, 116, 117, 133
    Urban Art/graffiti, 58, 79
    wayfinding sign, 184
Columbus, Ohio
    miscellaneous signs, 16, 17, 115, 118
    neon signs, 166, 167
commissioned artwork, 58, 60, 74, 104-105
Crawford's Bar & Grill (Sioux Falls, SD), 3
culture, local, 194, 196, 198-200, 200
    graffiti and, 56, 58, 60
    hand-lettered signs and, 85, 106, 107
    manhole covers and, 38
    murals and, 74
    neon signs and, 152, 168
    sign design and, 113, 132
    wayfinding signs and, 172, 174, 180
    See also specific cities
Cuyahoga Falls, Ohio
    hand-lettered sign, 95
    miscellaneous signs, 10, 131
    neon signs, 150, 157, 167
    Urban Art/graffiti, 79
    water company cover, 50
    wayfinding sign, 185

Fairey, Shepard, 68
Fillmore Theater (Miami, FL), 125
floor signs, 28-31
Fredericksburg, Virginia
    hand-lettered signs, 88, 100
    industrial typography, 127
    manhole covers and storm drain plaque, 38, 41, 45
    miscellaneous signs, 31, 134
    neon signs, 144, 145, 157
Frick & Lindsay Building (Pittsburgh, PA), 14

ghost signs, 6-27, 57, 113
    advertisers, 11

    atop buildings, 12-13
    common locations, 27
    painting/production methods, 21
    See also specific cities
Gillette and Hovis, 11
Gimenez (GG), Gabriel, 65
graffiti, 56-73
    artists, 61-65, 81
    See also specific cities; Street Art; Urban Art
Greenville, South Carolina
    hand-lettered signs, 95
    industrial typography, 126
    manhole covers and storm drain plaque, 38, 41, 46, 49, 51
    miscellaneous signs, 15, 23, 31
    wayfinding sign, 186
Greer, South Carolina
    hand-lettered signs, 93, 94, 95
    industrial typography, 126, 127, 202
    wayfinding sign, 179

hand-lettered signs, 57, 84-109
    artists, 86
    miscellaneous, 84-88, 90-93, 95, 97, 99-105, 107-109
    restaurant and bar, 83, 87, 89, 92, 96, 106
    service and repair shop, 91, 93, 94
    type choice and message, 86
    weathered, 102
    See also specific cities
Hudson, Ohio, 83, 89

industrial typography, 126-128

kerning, 132, 134, 182, 184
KiMo Theater (Albuquerque, NM), 152, 154
Kress buildings, 32-34

Lincoln Theater (Miami, FL), 125

manhole covers, 37-43, 51
    telephone company, 42-43
    typefaces, 38
    water company, 48-51
    weathered/deteriorating, 52-53
    See also specific cities; storm drain plaques
Massin, 72
Miami, Florida, 2, 33, 60-67, 81, 125, 194, 195, 201
    hand-lettered signs, 89, 100
    miscellaneous signs, 31, 116, 119, 122, 131, 137
    neon signs, 142-143, 144, 148, 168, 194
    Urban Art/graffiti and murals, 60-67, 71, 72, 74, 80-81, 194, 195, 205
    wayfinding signs, 177, 181, 186, 189
    Wynwood, 60, 65, 106

murals, 74-78, 205
   See also specific cities; Street Art; Urban Art

Nashville, Tennessee
   hand-lettered signs, 89, 94, 96
   manhole cover, 40
   miscellaneous signs, 9, 15, 22, 29, 112, 117, 133
   murals, 75
   neon signs, 151, 164, 168
   wayfinding signs, 175, 181
National Register of Historic Places, 14, 32, 121, 125, 152
neon signs, 57, 113, 141-143, 166, 168-169
   hotel and motel, 144, 148-149
   miscellaneous, 144-151, 167
   restaurant and bar, 143, 144, 156-165
   theater, 152-155
   See also specific cities
New Haven, Connecticut, 2, 198
   floor sign, 31
   manhole covers and storm drain plaque, 41, 46, 50
   neon signs, 159, 162
   Urban Art/graffiti and mural, 73, 78
   wayfinding signs, 176, 177
New York City
   hand-lettered signs, 88, 96
   industrial typography, 127
   miscellaneous signs, 22, 31, 113, 115, 118, 119, 122, 123, 133, 139, 202
   neon signs, 144, 156
   Urban Art/graffiti, 56-57
   wayfinding signs, 173, 176, 177, 181, 185, 187
Niagara Mohawk Building (Syracuse, NY), 121

Ohio Theatre (Cleveland, OH), 152
Orlando, Florida, 2, 14, 32, 192, 194
   hand-lettered sign, 94
   manhole covers, 38, 41, 42, 43
   miscellaneous signs, 12, 14, 31, 112, 120, 133, 192
   wayfinding signs, 177
Orpheum Theaters, 124

Paramount Theater (Boston, MA), 152, 153
Peninsula, Ohio
   miscellaneous signs, 122, 176
   neon sign, 162
Phoenix, Arizona, 25
Pittsburgh, Pennsylvania, 14
   hand-lettered sign, 94
   miscellaneous signs, 8, 14, 21, 24, 26, 27, 120, 122, 123, 139
   neon signs, 151, 154, 164, 168
   Urban Art/graffiti, 58
   wayfinding signs, 183, 186
Powers, Steve, 104

RETNA, 61
Richmond, Virginia, 2, 98-99, 124
   hand-lettered signs, 90, 97, 98-99, 102
   manhole covers, 41, 53
   miscellaneous signs, 7, 18, 23, 24, 112, 117, 134, 136, 196
   murals, 77
   neon signs, 151, 159
Richmond Dairy Company building, 98-99
Roa, 64
Rone, 62-63

Salem, Ohio, 18, 168
San Antonio, Texas, 2, 32, 34, 152, 155, 192, 194
   hand-lettered signs, 85, 94, 97, 103, 106
   industrial typography, 128
   manhole covers and storm drain plaques, 41, 42, 43, 44, 46, 48, 51, 52
   miscellaneous signs, 7, 8, 18, 31, 118, 133, 139, 193
   neon signs, 144, 149, 152, 155, 160, 162, 163, 166
   Urban Art/graffiti, 59
   wayfinding signs, 179, 182, 185, 186
San Francisco, California, 124
   manhole covers and storm drain plaques, 37, 45, 46, 51
   miscellaneous signs, 31, 115, 122, 134, 135, 202
   neon signs, 145, 146, 149, 151, 152, 160, 163, 164
   Urban Art/graffiti, 59, 69, 79
   wayfinding signs, 176, 180, 183, 184, 186, 187, 189
sans serif type, 28, 38, 52, 156, 174, 184-187
Scarbrough Building (Austin, TX), 130
script type, 28, 99, 117, 156, 184
serif type, 28, 38, 99, 152
signage, miscellaneous
   bank and insurance company, 114-115
   double-rail mounted, 123
   drugstore/pharmacy, 137
   florist, 111, 116
   funeral home, 132
   jewelry store, 134-135
   memorable/successful, 113, 132-133
   municipal and utility company, 121, 122, 131
   museum and library, 112, 120
   restaurant, 136, 138-139
   size requirements, 113
   theater, 124-125
   three-dimensional, 134-135
   See also specific cities and types of signs; industrial typography; typefaces; typography
signwriters, 21
Sioux Falls, South Dakota, 2, 3, 124, 199
   Convention & Visitors Bureau, 199
   hand-lettered sign, 93
   manhole cover and storm drain plaques, 40, 44, 45, 46
   miscellaneous signs, 10, 18, 19, 25, 28, 112, 117, 119, 120, 123, 132, 199

neon signs, 145, 149, 152, 157, 162
   wayfinding sign, 189
St. Louis, Missouri, 26
stencil art, 72
storm drain plaques, 44-47
Street Art, 56, 57
   See also graffiti; Urban Art
street banners, 188, 189
street signs. *See* wayfinding signs
Syracuse, New York, 2, 12, 121
   hand-lettered signs, 104-105
   industrial typography, 128
   manhole cover, 40
   miscellaneous signs, 6, 10, 12, 14, 15, 23, 31, 121, 138
   Urban Art/graffiti, 70, 71
   wayfinding signs, 177, 178, 188, 189

Tinker Building (Orlando, FL), 14
typefaces, 20, 52, 102, 117, 132, 174, 184
   See also sans serif type; script type; serif type
typography
   ghost and floor signs, 7, 11, 12, 28
   graffiti, 61
   local culture and, 1, 2, 57, 113, 196
   manhole covers, 38
   Massin, 72
   versus hand lettering, 85
   vintage signs, 16
   wayfinding signs, 184, 188
   See also industrial typography; sans serif type; script type; serif type; typefaces

Urban Art, 56
   See also specific cities; graffiti; murals; Street Art

Vermont Building (Boston, MA), 12, 13

walldogs, 21
wayfinding, 57, 113, 172
wayfinding signs, 172-187
   arrows and manicules, 173, 178-179
   city-specific design, 174, 180-181
   parking, 173, 174-177
   property line and private property, 182
   street names and numbers, 173, 183, 184-185
   transportation, 181-182
   See also specific cities; street banners
Wilson Building (Syracuse, NY), 12
Wooster, Ohio, 15

Yale University buildings, type treatment on, 198
Youngstown, Ohio, 35

More Great Titles from HOW Books

An Illustrated Journey

By Danny Gregory

Discover the artistic ideas behind the art journal pages of more than 40 famous and up-and-coming artists. Danny Gregory provides you with insights into private travel journals, helping you find artistic inspiration of your own. In each essay, the artist discusses experiences, materials and techniques alongside images shared from their personal art journals. If you love to travel and you love to create, then you'll love the inspiration provided in the pages of An Illustrated Journey.

Creative Workshop

By David Sherwin

Designers can often struggle to find creative inspiration because of tight deadlines and demanding workloads. So if you want to perform your best, then you need to exercise your creativity! Creative Workshop helps you do just that. Packed with 80 unique creative-thinking exercises that utilize all kinds of media and range in time limits (we know how rare free time can be), this book can help give your brain the creative workout it needs to stay sharp.

D30: Exercises for Designers

By Jim Krause

D30 contains thirty exercises designed to develop and strengthen the creative powers of graphic designers, artists and photographers in a variety of intriguing and fun ways. What will you need to begin? Not much. Most of the book's step-by-step projects call for setting aside an hour or two, rolling up your sleeves and grabbing art supplies that are probably already stashed somewhere in your home or studio—things like pens, drawing and watercolor paper, paints, scissors and glue. Try these hands-on exercises to unleash your creativity and get unblocked!

Find these books and many others at **MyDesignShop.com** or your local bookstore.

SPECIAL OFFER FROM HOW BOOKS!
You can get 15% off your entire order at MyDesignShop.com! All you have to do is go to www.howdesign.com/howbooks-offer and sign up for our free e-newsletter on graphic design. You'll also get a free digital download of HOW magazine.

For more news, tips and articles, follow us at **Twitter.com/HOWbrand**

For behind-the-scenes information and special offers, become a fan at **Facebook.com/HOWmagazine**

For visual inspiration, follow us at **Pinterest.com/HOWbrand**